The Handyman

Ronald Harwood's plays include *The Dresser, Interpreters, Another Time, Reflected Glory* and *Taking Sides*. He is also the author of *Sir Donald Wolfit, CBE: His Life and Work in the Unfashionable Theatre*, and a history of the theatre, *All the World's a Stage*. He is the editor of *The Faber Book of the Theatre*. He was visitor in Theatre at Balliol College, Oxford, was President of English PEN from 1990 to 1993 and has been President of International PEN since 1993. He was made Chevalier de l'Ordre des Arts et des Lettres in 1996.

RONALD HARWOOD

The Handyman

faber and faber

First published in 1996
by Faber and Faber Limited
3 Queen Square London WC1N 3AU

Typeset by Faber and Faber Ltd

Printed in England by
Antony Rowe Ltd, Eastbourne,
England

© Ronald Harwood, 1996

Ronald Harwood is hereby identified as author of this
work in accordance with Section 77 of the Copyright,
Designs and Patents Act 1988

All professional and amateur rights in this play are strictly reserved and
applications for permission to perform them must be made in advance,
before rehearsals begin, to: Judy Daish Associates, 2 St Charles Place,
London W10 6EG. No performance may be given without a licence being
first obtained.

*This book is sold subject to the condition that it shall not, by way of trade
or otherwise, be lent, resold, hired out or otherwise circulated without the
publisher's prior consent in any form of binding or cover other than that in
which it is published and without a similar condition including this condition being imposed on the subsequent purchaser*

A CIP record for this book
is available from the British Library

ISBN 0-571-19041-3

For
Rachel and Kevin Billington

*I am deeply grateful to Roderick Gilchrist, the deputy edi-
tor of the* Mail on Sunday, *for introducing me to his
newspaper's chief crime reporter, Chester Stern, who gave
generously of his time and expertise. He, in turn, intro-
duced me to a senior member, now retired, of the
Scotland Yard War Crimes Squad, who wishes to remain
anonymous. We spent many hours together and without
him the play could not have been written. I want also to
thank the Hon. Greville Janner QC MP, Shimon Cohen,
Lionel Bloch, Alexander Tkachenko, Professor Colin
Tatz, Charles Hartley-Davis and Miranda Fricker who
were of great help in a variety of areas. I must make clear
that none of them has read the play or attended
rehearsals. Any errors and inaccuracies are, therefore,
entirely my responsibility.*

Characters

Cressida Field, 35
Roman Kozachenko, 78
Julian Field, 33
Detective Inspector Washbourne, 42
Detective Constable Mather, 31
Marian Stone, 36
Nikita Fedorenko, 82
Sister Sophia, 75

The play takes place on the terrace of a house in the
Sussex countryside and in an interview room in Scotland
Yard, London.

The **Handyman** was first performed at the Minerva
Theatre, Chichester, on 19 September 1996 with the following cast:

Cressida Field Kate Lynn-Evans
Roman Kozachenko Frank Finlay
Julian Field Hugh Bonneville
Marian Stone Francesca Hunt
DI Washbourne Nick Stringer
DC Mather David Garvey
Nikita Fedorenko Allan Surtees
Sister Sophia Sheila Burrell

Directed by Christopher Morahan
Designed by John Gunter
Lighting by Mick Hughes
Sound by Tom Lishman

Act One

The terrace of a house in the Sussex countryside. A blazing July day. 9 a.m. There are entrances from the house and from the garden.

Cressida Field, dressed neatly and conventionally, is seated at a table under a parasol. She is consulting text books, making notes.

Roman Kozachenko enters. He is old but is surprisingly vigorous. He wears an earth-stained apron and a battered straw hat.

Roman Is done.

Cressida You wrapped her in something.

Roman Sure.

Cressida What?

Roman Pillow-case.

Cressida Not one of our good ones? ↗ main concern

Roman No. Old one. Mine. I go tell Mr Julian I have done this. He is walking?

Cressida Yes, but I'll tell him. He'll blub, of course.

Roman Blub?

Cressida Yes.

Roman What means blub?

Cressida You know what blub means.

Roman I never heard this word.

Cressida Of course you have.

Roman Blub, no, never.

Cressida To blub. To cry. Unmanfully.

Roman Ah. I blub also. When I dig grave, I blub.

Cressida Yes, you and Mr Julian are very soft-hearted.

Roman Is good, blub, no? Is good?

She returns to her books.

I make her name on wood.

Cressida Not a cross.

Roman No, no. I take flat piece wood. This size – (*He indicates.*) I make two coats white paint, weather-proof, black letters for name. Rosy. You spell R-o-s-y, yes?

Cressida No. R-o-s-i-e.

Roman No problem. I put also date. Also in black letters. How old she was?

Cressida Eleven.

Roman I put also age. You come see later?

Julian Field enters from the house. He is conventionally handsome and dressed in casual chic.

Julian What's going on in the lane?

Cressida What?

Julian Police.

Cressida In our lane?

Julian Dozens of them. At least two cars. And a mini-bus.

Cressida Are you pulling my leg?

Julian No, they're there, I promise you. Go and look.

Cressida What are they doing?

Julian Just parked.

Cressida Where?

Julian At the fork. They had thermos flasks and sandwiches. Like a works' outing.

Cressida Did you ask them what they were doing there?

Julian No. I just walked by.

Cressida Probably the Miltons. *overbearing?*

Julian That's exactly what I thought. You remember I said to you the other day? Nobody knows what Milton does, nobody knows where he comes from or how he got his money. You remember me saying that?

Cressida Yes –

Julian Romka, you've never found out anything about him, have you?

Roman No.

Julian There you are. Lives like a king, a Roller, a chauffeur, but where does the money come from?

A pleasant silence.

You want something, Romka?

Cressida He's just buried Rosie.

Julian blubs.

Julian God, I loved that bloody cat. *Oh.*

Cressida We'll get another.

Julian I don't know if I can go through it again. (*He tries not to blub.*)

dramatic

3

Roman I blub also.

Julian What d'you mean you blub also? I wasn't blubbing. I was just moved that's all. (*He collects himself.*) Jesus, I'm glad we didn't have children.

Silence.

Roman You want come see grave?

Julian No. Not today. Perhaps tomorrow. By the way, the hedge by the barn needs doing. I haven't walked that way for a couple of weeks. It's in a dreadful state. You think you can manage?

Roman Sure.

Julian Do you want me to get help?

Roman No, I manage. No problem.

Cressida It's awfully hot, Romka.

Roman I manage. I got hat.

Julian That hat's about as much use as a tennis racket in a rainstorm.

Roman I have this hat forty years.

Julian It looks it. And it can't be forty years, it would have disintegrated by now –

Roman Major give me, I remember –

Cressida *I* gave it to you. *After* Daddy died. That's eight years ago.

Roman Is good hat.

Julian Let me get someone in to help you with the hedge. What's Crowther's lad called?

Roman Philip.

4

Julian I'll get Philip in. He's a good, strong lad. Crowther won't mind.

Roman No, I do hedge myself. I prefer. Old times takes one day. Now, two. No problem.

Cressida Then you must promise to take one of Mr Julian's hats from the stand. You can't work in that, you'll get sun stroke. → so she *does* care, or appearances?

Julian Poor Rosie. I really, truly adored her. She loved you, Romka.

Roman I love her also. Very independent. Like my Maureen. → problematic?

Cressida Yes, but rather more gentle.

Awkward pause.

Roman I make start on hedge.

Cressida Take one of Mr Julian's hats –

Roman goes.

Julian God, he's an obstinate old bugger.

Cressida He always was. And his memory's going. Forty years ago. As if a straw hat could last forty years.

Julian He's drinking again.

Cressida No, I'm sure not –

Julian Yes, he is. Last night, when I was sitting out here, listening to *The Magic Flute*, I heard him talking to himself at the top of his voice. And he only used to do that when he was pissed. I know exactly when it started again. Just after Easter. When I began taking Fridays off. The week after Good Friday. I went for a walk and heard him. And again last weekend, Sunday night, ranting and raving. Pissed.

Cressida Why didn't you tell me?

Julian Because you'd try to stop him. He's an old man. Let him get pissed if he wants to. He's lonely. Let him talk to himself.

Cressida He's probably talking to Maureen.

Julian bursts out laughing.

What's so funny?

Julian Do you realize what you've just said?

Cressida Yes, I said he's probably talking to Maureen.

Julian I said he's talking to himself. You said he's talking to Maureen. Maureen's been dead five years so he's talking to himself, isn't he?

Cressida Yes, I see – (*She laughs, too, but not as heartily.*) He misses Maureen.

Julian I don't. She was a bitch. Made his life a misery.

Cressida I don't mind him drinking. He's the sweetest drunk I know.

Julian Except when he feels sorry for himself. (*Breathes deeply.*) What a wonderful, splendid, life-enhancing, magnificent, beautiful day! You know the best decision I ever made, Cress? Taking Fridays off. Best decision I ever made.

Cressida Where did you walk?

Julian All the way down to the village.

Cressida Did you?

Julian I can't tell you how glorious it was. The country-side at its best. From the top of Payne's Hill I could see all the way to the Castle. It looked like one of those sentimental paintings –

6

Cressida Chocolate box –

Julian Like a setting for an opera, perfect but artificial. And there were these lovely, evocative sounds. A dog barking. A small aeroplane droning somewhere overhead. Bees buzzing, of course. I couldn't see her but I heard Mrs Babington-Wells calling, 'Good morning, vicar,' and the vicar calling back, 'Good morning, Mrs Babington-Wells.' England, my England. Made me laugh out loud.

Cressida Why should that make you laugh?

Julian I don't know but it did. And then, coming back, seeing those police cars really upset me. They were so sinister. And in our lane. I wonder what Milton's been up to?

Cressida returns to her books and notes.

How's it going?

Cressida Painfully.

Julian What's it this week?

Cressida Same as last week.

Julian Remind me.

Cressida 'How far can the law alone deliver gender equality?'

Julian Wouldn't know where to begin.

Cressida I shouldn't have chosen this. There was another title they gave. I think I would have found it easier. (*Searches for a note.*) Yes. 'If the personal is political, should the law intervene in the private domain?'

Julian Easier. I see. I consider myself not unintelligent, but, d'you know, I didn't understand a word of what you've just said –

His mobile telephone, which is in his back pocket, rings. He answers it.

(into telephone; immediately begins to pace) Yes? *(Listens.)* Eddie, yes? *(Listens.)* Christ. What's happening to the Dax? How far is it off? *(Listens.)* So how bad is our Jefferson deal looking? How far are we out on this? *(Listens.)* Twenty-two million Deutsche Marks! Look, Steve sold this idea to me. Jefferson is his fucking problem. We need to cut our losses, tell him to pay market for five hundred Dec At-The-Money puts. *(Listens but interrupts almost immediately.)* No. Use Carlo, he's cheaper. Market for five hundred.

He listens and, while he does so, Detective Inspector Washbourne and Detective Constable Mather enter from the garden. Cressida sees them but Julian, at first, doesn't notice them. Washbourne indicates that he will wait for Julian to finish.

(continuing into telephone) I don't want any of our clients left out of this. Beckmans were talking about this last week. Cover up to fifty on the Decs ninety-sevens. Also check the cash-future basis. I don't want to be left out in the cold on the spread. Tell George to keep an eye on it. If it opens to more than eight ticks, get George basket trading. *(He notices Washbourne and Mather.)* I don't want to be left out on this one. *(Listens.)* Okay. *(Puts away his mobile, sees the two newcomers.)* Yes?

Washbourne has a deceptively gentle manner.

Washbourne We rang the bell at the front door but nobody answered.

Julian What do you want?

Washbourne Mr –?

Julian Field. Julian Field. Who are *you*?

Washbourne (*to Cressida*) And you are –?

Cressida I'm his wife.

Washbourne and Mather produce warrant cards.

Washbourne Police. Detective Inspector Washbourne and this is D. C. Mather, War Crimes Squad, Scotland Yard.

Puzzled silence.

Julian What squad?

Washbourne War Crimes. You have an employee, living on these premises, Mr Roman Kozachenko?

Julian and Cressida Yes –?

Washbourne Could we see him, please?

Julian What's this about?

Washbourne We'd like to see Mr Kozachenko. If you could just ask him to join us. I'd prefer you to be present, sir. Would he be in his quarters?

Julian I don't know where he is –

Mather He has a flat above the garage, doesn't he?

Cressida No, no, he won't be there, he's probably down by the hedge, what's he done?

Julian How did you know he has the flat above the garage?

Washbourne If we could just see him, sir –

Julian Wait a moment, wait a moment, you can't just come barging in here and start ordering us about –

Washbourne As I said, sir, we did ring the front door bell –

Cressida I asked Romka to fix it, we can't hear it out here –

Julian Never mind fixing the bell, what's this about, what squad, what Scotland Yard squad –?

Washbourne War Crimes, sir. If we could just see Mr Kozachenko –

Cressida Best to get him, Jules –

Julian hesitates, then goes. Washbourne nods to Mather who immediately follows Julian. Awkward silence.

Cressida There are more of you, aren't there?

Washbourne Yes.

Cressida In our lane?

Washbourne Yes.

Cressida This is serious, isn't it? I mean, it's not a parking offence –

She tries to laugh but can't; no response from Washbourne.

Are you sure you have the right house?

Julian and Mather return with Roman.

Mather I believe this is the gentleman, guv. I've already identified myself.

Washbourne (*showing his identification*) I'm Detective Inspector Washbourne of the War Crimes Squad, Scotland Yard. You are?

Roman (*indicating Mather*) I tell him already –

Washbourne Tell me.

Roman I am Roman Kozachenko.

Washbourne And you were born where, sir?

Roman I was born in Starivka, Ukraine, December 2nd,

1917. But I am British citizen.

Washbourne I wonder if you would mind also telling me your parents' names, sir –

Julian What is this? We're entitled to know what the hell all this is about.

Washbourne (*to Julian*) Information has been received which involves Mr Kozachenko in war crimes committed in the Ukraine in 1941.

Julian War crimes, what war crimes?

Washbourne Murder. The murder of eight hundred and seventeen Jews. (*to Roman*) Your parents' names, if you don't mind, sir –

Roman Father, Ivan. Mother, Olya.

Washbourne and Mather exchange a brief, satisfied look.

Washbourne Mr Kozachenko, I have a warrant here to search your living quarters. (*to Julian*) The warrant also includes your house, sir. (*He hands the warrant to Julian.*)

Julian You're going to search my house? What for? I haven't done anything! How dare you have a search warrant for my house?

Cressida Our house –

Blackout.

Light on.
The same. Some hours later.
Julian, Cressida and Roman watching Washbourne signing a document which he hands to Roman. Mather is at Washbourne's elbow.

Washbourne Mr Kozachenko, here is a receipt of the

articles we have taken from your quarters.

Gives him the receipt; Mather hands Washbourne another sheet which he also signs and then hands to Julian.

And here's your receipt, Mr Field.

Cressida hurries to Julian and together they study the receipt.

Cressida You've taken Daddy's photograph albums. And his War Diary. →so this house was inherited by Cress?

Julian goes to Roman and studies his receipt.

Washbourne It'll all be returned to you in due course.

Cressida What do you mean, 'in due course'? It's our property –

Julian Why have you taken his passport? This is ridiculous, he's not going anywhere – (*Notices something else.*) Pay book? Pay book? What pay book? We don't write down what we pay him in a pay book! I get it! This isn't about war crimes. This is something to do with tax, isn't it? Isn't that what it's all about? Will you please do us the courtesy of answering at least *one* question? Isn't this about tax avoidance or tax evasion –?

Mather His army pay book, sir.

Julian His army pay book? (*to Roman*) You've kept your army pay book all these years?

Cressida Superintendent –

Washbourne Inspector –

Cressida Inspector, whatever. This is a nightmare, you know, an absolute nightmare. How many Jews did you say were murdered?

Washbourne Eight hundred and seventeen.

Cressida In 1941. →so that makes it irrelevant?* set in 90's

Washbourne Mr Kozachenko, we will now be returning to London to examine the items we have taken and to make further enquiries. That may take a little time. When we are ready, we will invite you to attend an interview at Scotland Yard. We will also want to interview you and Mrs Field, sir –

Julian Who the hell do you think you are? Invite him to attend an interview, you'll want to interview us? See yourself as some sort of moral force, do you? Suddenly on the side of right, are we? Tired of convicting the innocent, are we? No, oh, no, on to the real thing now, are we? Do you know last year my car was broken into in Chester Row –

Cressida (*trying to stop him*) Jules –

Julian (*unstoppable*) – that's in Belgravia, you know, in broad daylight, my radio taken, in Chester Row, London, sw1, where the hell were you then? Fitting up some poor black bastard in Brixton, were you? Come here, high and mighty, search warrants blazing, poking about our house, turning things upside down as if we were criminals, behaving like the bloody Gestapo, I'm going to report this to my MP, what are we living in now, a police state? I am simply not going to put up with this –

His mobile rings. He answers it.

(*into mobile*) Not now! (*He clicks off the mobile but has run out of steam.*)

Washbourne (*continuing to Roman as if there was no interruption*) And when we do interview you, Mr Kozachenko, I strongly advise you to have a solicitor present. Good morning, or rather, good afternoon.

[handwritten margin note: all hot air even if he's politically correct. omg Julian's a hipster.]

13

He and Mather go.

Cressida That was stupid of you, Jules, why antagonize them?

Julian Why? Why? Because I felt like it, that's why.

Restless silence.

I need a drink.

Cressida Yes, please.

Julian Romka?

Roman Please.

Julian is about to go into the house when Roman breaks down and cries quietly.

Julian Romka, we're going to fight this. We're not going to take this lying down. We're going to fight these bastards.

He goes into the house. Cressida goes to Roman, puts an arm round him, comforts him.

Cressida Please don't cry, Romka, dear, darling Romka, please don't cry.

Roman I am not this man they want.

Cressida Did you have any idea they were going to come this morning?

Roman No. But I – (*He breaks off.*)

Cressida What?

Roman Few months ago, Easter time, when I went to London, to Club, I heard, people say me police asking questions, here, there –

Cressida Asking questions about you? Why didn't you tell us?

Roman Is not me, Cressy, they have wrong man, I am not this man. I tell him, this Inspector, but he say me nothing. I say him you have wrong man, I say him over and over –

Cressida And he said nothing at all?

Roman I ask him, what murder, what Jews? Where, how, what? He don't answer, just make his men search, up, down, behind bed, ask for keys, all he wants is keys, where keys, where I keep things? They open drawers, cupboards, tool box, I ask him, why? What? He don't answer. I tell him, is not me! This is not right, Cressy. I am old man.

Brief silence. ⟶ courtroom tactic – negative reaction to crime transfers to accused

Cressida How many Jews did he say were murdered?

No response. Julian returns carrying a tray with two bottles and three glasses.

Julian (*to Roman*) There's no vodka, but I found this stuff I brought back from Sweden –

Roman No problem –

Julian pours scotch for himself and Cressida and hands the other bottle and third glass to Roman. They drink.

Cressida I'll take you to Mass on Sunday, Romka.

Roman Very good. Thank you.

Cressida Will you come, too, Jules?

Julian No.

Silence. They drink.

Cressida Oh God –

Julian What?

Cressida It's gone straight to my head. It's after one, I'm starving, I'll go and make lunch.

Roman I make.

Cressida No, Romka –

But he goes. Silence.

How many Jews did he say were murdered?

Julian What's it matter how many Jews? They've got the wrong man, that's what matters. Romka? It's unthinkable –

Cressida I think he said eight hundred –

Julian Something like that –

Cressida The whole world's spinning –

Julian Don't drink any more –

Julian refills their glasses.

Cressida What are we going to do?

Julian We're going to take advice. Legal advice. I'll call Rodney – yes, wait a moment – I had an idea –

Cressida Rodney isn't the man for this –

Julian But he'll know who is – (*Mobile rings; he answers it. Into mobile*) Yes? (*Listens.*) You tell George from me, if he screws up on this I will personally detach his private parts from the rest of his body with my own bare hands. Got it? Good. Tell him. (*Switches off mobile.*) What were we saying?

Cressida I can't remember – wait a moment – I asked about how many Jews – and you said – what did you say –?

Julian I said – I said – it's gone – damnation –

Cressida You said something about Rodney –

Julian Right, and you said Rodney's no good to us. I had

(margin note: sudden switch of notes)

16

an idea and then the bloody phone rang – what was it? – I was on to something – wait a moment – I'll remember – legal advice – we need legal advice – didn't that little twerp say something about having a solicitor – when he interviews Romka – and I thought – war crimes, Jews murdered, yes, wait a moment, we get a lawyer, of course, of course, yes, I remember now, I had a terrific idea. We don't just get any lawyer. Of course! It's obvious. We get a Jewish lawyer!

He smiles triumphantly. She downs another drink.
Blackout.

Lights on.
A few days later. Early evening.
Marian Stone, lithe, relaxed, attractive, trendily dressed, stands alone on the terrace, admiring the view. After a moment, Julian enters from the garden.

Julian I'm sorry, I can't find her. She's not feeling terribly well. These last few days have been brutal. As you can imagine. She's gone for a stroll but I can't see her. If she'd only carry a mobile, I could call her. (*He smiles.*) She knows you're coming –

Marian Perhaps I could meet Mr Kozachenko.

Julian Cressida thought the three of us ought to talk first. We've each made a list of things we want to ask you. (*He takes a piece of paper from his pocket.*) Is that all right?

Marian Of course.

Julian (*awkward pause*) Refreshment? Champagne, scotch –?

Marian No, thank you, have to keep a clear head.

Julian It's good of you to come down.

No response.

Do you know exactly what they're going to hit him with, evidence, witnesses –?

Marian No.

Awkward silence.

Julian These – these events took place more than fifty years ago.

Marian Yes, they did.

Julian Then why don't they just forget about them?

Marian Because they've changed the law. Of course, there's never been a statute of limitation for murder. And until this new War Crimes Act, British courts had jurisdiction only over British citizens who had committed manslaughter or murder abroad, but didn't have jurisdiction over people who may now be British citizens, or who may now live here and have done for some time, if the allegations relate to events before they became British citizens, or before they came to live here. The new Act changed all that. You see?

Julian Yes. (*He doesn't.*) Is this sort of case a speciality of yours?

Marian This sort of case?

Julian War crimes –

Marian I don't think war crimes are anyone's speciality, Mr Field, except for very old men and United Nations employees.

He regards her for a moment, smiles.

Julian You don't look Jewish.

Marian Is that meant to be a compliment?

Julian No, no, it's just – I – no, not at all –

Marian I'll put you at your ease. I don't look Jewish, whatever that may mean, because I'm not Jewish.

Julian Oh.

Marian But I'm the next best thing, I'm married to one. I always get that in as soon as I can. Saves any embarrassment should anyone say anything untoward later. Which I'm sure you won't.

Julian I thought a Jewish solicitor, in this case, would be rather a good idea. I consulted my man. Rodney Butler. He thought it was a good idea, too. What went wrong?

Marian You think something's gone wrong, do you?

Julian No, no, no, no, no, I put that badly, I meant – no, no, no –

Marian I seem to make you nervous. Why?

Julian No, no, no, no. I just wondered – I mean – how did they get hold of you? to say the least

Marian Yes, you do put things badly. I'll explain how they got hold of me. Apparently, your Mr Butler tried several people. All absolutely refused to have anything to do with it. This morning he tried us. One of our senior partners, Alan Ross, Jewish, said he wouldn't touch it with a barge pole. But he's a conscientious old stick. And a good lawyer. He talked to me. I do a lot of criminal work, the allegations relate to special interests of mine, so here I am.

Julian I didn't know solicitors could refuse to take a case.

Marian Solicitors can, barristers can't.

Uneasy pause.

Julian We're Catholics. 'Carthlicks'. We go to 'Mahss'.

I'm a convert. A trifle lapsed. My wife's the genuine article. So is Mr Kozachenko. That's part of the background. My late father-in-law – well, we better wait for Cressida, she'll tell you more. And you're a criminal lawyer.

Marian Do you try very hard to be insulting or does it come naturally? *I love her.*

Julian Sorry, sorry, sorry, but, now this *is* meant to be a compliment. You don't look like a lawyer. You look so – so – fit.

No response.

You go to the gym, I suppose, you do all that, do you?

Marian Yes.

Julian What, twice, three times a week –?

Marian Twice.

Julian Weights, running, bicycling, all that –?

Marian Yes, all that. And self-defence.

Julian Self-defence, really? What, judo, kung-fu –?

Marian No. Kick boxing.

Julian Kick boxing, I see.

Awkward pause.

I'm in money. Derivatives. (*Goes to garden entrance, looks out, returns.*) A lot of people think that's immoral.

Marian A lot of people think what's immoral?

Julian Making money out of money. You don't, do you?

Marian No, I don't think it's immoral, but you obviously do.

Julian tries to laugh but fails.

Julian My wife's studying for a degree – late – I mean, she's older than me – I was at Bristol – read history – she never went to university, so now – adult education – I don't know what you call it exactly – but I do admire her – it's a lot of work – no time for much else. Gender Studies. That's her degree course. Gender Studies.

Another awkward pause.

I take Fridays off.

Marian It's all right for some.

Julian Today's a bonus. Two days off this week. Every cloud has a – (*Doesn't finish; goes and looks out again; returns.*) This has all come as a terrible shock.

Marian I'm sure.

Julian We live our lives oblivious, as it were. During the week, Cressida's here, studying, writing her unintelligible essays, running the place, Romka – that's Mr Kozachenko, his name's Roman but we call him Romka – he's her only company. I go up to the City, work like hell, spend all day on the phone making a few bob, and then this comes along. Something one's never thought about. War crimes. Scotland Yard. It's like suddenly being told you've got a terminal illness. You can't think of anything else. Ordinary, everyday concerns become trivial. We buried our cat last week. That was the biggest event in our lives. Which reminds me, I must visit her grave. Was it last week? It feels like last century. We're supposed to be going to Glyndebourne on Thursday. *The Magic Flute.* It seems utterly ridiculous. And we're great opera buffs. Go all the time. Now, it's the last thing I want to do. (*He regards her for a moment.*) Do you like the opera?

Marian No.

Julian Oh.

Marian I prefer the theatre.

Julian You don't.

Marian Yes, I do.

Julian But nobody goes to the theatre any more.

Marian Always seems pretty full when I'm there.

Julian Not the opera?

Marian No.

Julian But everybody goes to the opera.

Marian I don't.

She smiles. Awkward silence.

Julian About Mr Kozachenko.

Marian Yes?

Julian I'm determined to fight this to the finish.

No response.

I've known Romka all my married life, that's ten years now, and I tell you with absolute certainty that he is incapable of murder. My late father-in-law, who was a wonderful judge of character, believed Romka to be one of the few truly good men he had ever met. I second that. This whole business is just a dreadful mistake. Romka's an innocent man. My guess is, this is a case of mistaken identity like the one –

Cressida enters.

Cressy. (*Finding Marian's business card.*) Allow me to introduce Ms Marian Stone of Horton, Cooper and Ross. This is my wife, Cressida.

Marian and Cressida shake hands.

Cressida It's good of you to come down –

Julian Yes, I said that –

Cressida Have you offered Ms Stone –?

Marian I prefer Mrs Stone – (*Marian takes out papers from her briefcase.*)

Julian She doesn't want anything. (*He draws Cressida aside.*) She's not Jewish. Husband is.

Marian You want to talk to me –

Cressida I thought perhaps it would be a good idea if we could ask you some questions, we made lists – (*She goes to the table, finds her list.*)

Marian Of course –

Cressida We're so confused, totally in the dark. And then perhaps we could fill you in on the background. It may help –

Marian Yes, it may –

Cressida Do sit.

They all sit. Uneasy moment.

I'm rather envious of you.

Marian Why?

Cressida I would have loved to have read law. But my father was an invalid. And, ironically, my mother, who was perfectly healthy for most of her life, died first, when I was seventeen, just the moment I would have gone up to university, but someone had to look after Daddy, I mean, Romka – that's what we call Mr Kozachenko, his name's Roman but we call him Romka – he couldn't manage on his own, so it wasn't possible for me to – but, I'm working for a degree now, not law, Gender Studies –

Marian Yes, your husband told me –

Cressida I don't think he approves, do you, Julian?

Julian Of course I approve –

Cressida (*to Marian*) What university were you at?

Marian Oxford.

Cressida You read law?

Marian First I read philosophy, then I read law.

Julian Blimey.

Cressida You make me feel very inadequate –

Marian No, no, no, just means I'm good at exams, that's all. Mrs Field –

Cressida Cressida –

Marian I really do think we had better discuss the reason for my being here. And then I must talk to Mr Kozachenko. I need to get back to London tonight. I have a meeting early tomorrow morning.

Cressida Yes, yes, I'm sorry. Just let me collect my thoughts. (*She studies her list.*)

Julian Tell Cressy what you told me.

Marian About what?

Julian About the law and all that.

Cressida Yes, and can you tell us where these allegations come from, this information –?

Marian Obviously I haven't had much time to make enquiries or do any research, but, as far as I can ascertain, about ten years ago the Simon Wiesenthal Centre in Los Angeles produced a list of names which, they claimed, was a list of war criminals who were now living in Britain and had been doing so for many years. Another list was supplied by the embassy of the former Soviet Union. Mr Kozachenko's name appeared on both those lists. According to one of my police contacts, Mr Kozachenko's name also surfaced as a result of enquiries into similar matters made by the Australian and Canadian police. They passed it on to Scotland Yard. I have no idea what evidence Scotland Yard has to support the allegations.

Julian And we don't know where these murders were supposed to have taken place or any other details?

Marian I don't, but Scotland Yard does.

Cressida You said the government received the list ten years ago. Why wasn't he charged then?

Marian Because, as I explained to your husband –

Julian Julian –

Marian – the law didn't allow it. But the law's been changed. When these men from Eastern Europe entered Britain just after the war, they could not be prosecuted for war crimes because they were not British citizens when the alleged crimes were committed. That, in essence, is what the new Act changed. We can now prosecute them as we would any other British citizen. There is an element of what we lawyers call retrospective legislation of which I don't approve. But it's now the law. And that's why we're here.

Cressida It can't be right, can it, to pursue old men for a crime they're alleged to have committed more than fifty years ago?

Marian I'm not sure that's a good argument. If old men commit murder shouldn't they pay the penalty the same as anyone else? After all, murder is murder. And I don't think time has anything to do with it. Where do you draw the line? When do you stop bringing a murderer to justice? After five years? Ten, twenty? The morality of justice requires that wrong-doing is not condoned no matter how long ago it took place.

Julian Here's one of my questions. What's the point?

Marian Of what?

Julian Of a trial. Suppose Romka's put on trial and he's found guilty. All right. They send him to prison. But what's the point? Is he to be rehabilitated so that he can return to the community and lead – what's the phrase – a useful life? Or will they be locking him away so that he won't be able to repeat the offence?

Marian Good question. Do we punish or rehabilitate? But those are not the only reasons for a trial. It can be argued that a trial is as good a way as any of a society proclaiming the standards by which it lives. This trial, if we get that far, may demonstrate our society's revulsion to the crimes of which Mr Kozachenko and others may be accused. We don't, of course, yet know the particulars, but we can sure of one thing: the details, how the eight hundred and seventeen Jews were done to death, will be unbearable.

Cressida (*consulting her list*) And I suppose a trial can also be seen as a deterrent, can't it?

Julian Oh, Cressy, don't be silly. Nobody's going to start murdering Jews nowadays, are they? _spoken so casually_

Marian That's a moot point.

Brief silence.

Oddly enough, it's one of my other objections to all this.

Julian I don't understand.

Marian Airing these events may provide an impetus to Jew-baiting. Not that it ever needs much of an impetus. My husband's a journalist –

Julian Gerald Stone, of course –

Marian Yes. Whenever he's written on the subject he's received hate mail of the most extraordinary kind. Once, he wrote a piece critical of the Foreign Office in which he quoted a well-known remark. When the first news of the Holocaust was coming in, an official is reported to have said, 'Oh the Jews are always complaining.' The day after Gerald's article was published, the postman delivered a package. It contained shit.

Cressida Oh God, how awful –

Marian So these investigations, a trial, evidence, witnesses, arguments, may release the poison. And poison it is, but don't get me started on that, we'd be here all night. No. What I especially fear is something else. That those who deny the Holocaust ever happened will have a field day.

Julian Yes, but they're just nutters, aren't they?

Marian Some of them. Others are learned academics who have gone to great lengths to prove, scientifically, that the Holocaust is just another Jewish conspiracy. I have even heard it described as a Jewish fantasy.

Cressida That's obscene.

Marian Yes. And, of course, the two words, 'war crimes', are also obscene in their own modest way. They're the most economic justification for armed conflict I know. If you think about it, the simplicity is startling. War crimes. They tell you instantly that war's all right, that society accepts war as legal, but brands its excesses as criminal. Men and women can legally slaughter each other but only

she's a bit idealistic, meaning that she focuses on

27   philosophical principles

more than events

up to a point. All that in two words. Good, isn't it? (*Glances at her watch.*) Now, please tell me what happened here last Friday.

Julian The police had a search warrant and they took away a whole heap of stuff including Romka's passport, an old army pay book, I don't know what else, he has a receipt, but here's what they took from us. (*Hands Marian the receipt.*) You'll see there, my father-in-law's war diaries, some old photograph albums, letters and, evidently, a file labelled 'R. K.' but I don't ever remember seeing it. Do you, Cressy?

Cressida No, and I certainly don't know what's in it.

Marian When did Mr Kozachenko come to work here?

Cressida Before I was born. 1947, I think. My father was a major during the war, in Intelligence. He was a wonderful linguist, a classicist, actually, he took a First, at Cambridge, and he'd learned Russian. He was wounded. He'd gone for a walk in a wood. Somewhere in Germany. A sniper hit him twice. Once in the stomach, once in the knee. It seems he recovered rather quickly, or so they thought, and was posted to a prisoner of war camp near Rimini. A lot of Ukrainians were held there and for reasons I never quite understood many of them were allowed to come into Britain.

Marian And Mr Kozachenko was one of them.

Cressida Yes. We're Catholics. So were most of the Ukrainians. Romka's Catholic. And we've had a wonderful life as a result of him being here. He does everything for us. Cooks, sews, builds, digs, mends fences, drives the car, grows the most wonderful vegetables, and just look at the garden, he's a life-saver, nothing's too much trouble for him. In the camp, my father obviously took a shine to him and he became a sort of unofficial servant. Daddy hadn't really recovered from his wounds. I know because I remember a snap of Daddy in a wheelchair with Romka pushing him. In the camp. Near Rimini.

Marian Was that photograph in the album the police took?

Cressida I don't know, it could have been. I haven't looked at that album for years. When it was agreed the Ukrainians could enter Britain, my father either applied to the authorities or used his influence – everything's influence, isn't it? – and Romka came to live and work here. This house has been in the family for over a hundred years. So Daddy could manage on his various pensions and – (*Breaks off.*) He needed looking after. He tired easily. The wound in his stomach never properly healed. He wasn't married then. He married late. He met my mother in the fifties, 1958, I think. She was a nurse. She'd come to nurse him. I was born in 1960. Daddy was already 55.

Brief silence.

Romka's been a member of this family for fifty years. A lifetime. All my lifetime. He's been my nanny, mentor, friend and companion all my life. He's been a second father to me. I know him as well as I know anybody.

Julian But you can't help wondering, can you? How well does one ever know anybody?

Brief silence.

Cressida I haven't slept a night through since this began. In fact, I've hardly slept at all. In ordinary circumstances we lead quiet, orderly, predictable lives. Rather protected. Now, this. I've only ever thought about – these things in the most general terms, thought of them as a kind of pervasive horror of which the details are best left unknown. And then one tries to imagine the reality of evil, of cruelty, sadism, barbarism. One imagines oneself a victim. The words genocide, Holocaust, Final Solution, so easy to say, so difficult to comprehend. Was Romka capable of partaking in horror, I've asked myself over and over again? Is he a monster who has been living in our midst all these years? I say with absolute confidence, from my own intimate knowledge of him over many years, that he is incapable of cruelty. Romka is not evil.

a little bit of drama here too

Marian I wish you hadn't used that word.

Cressida What word?

Marian Evil. My husband and I often fight about whether the perpetrators were evil or not. I don't believe in evil. I have a very well-rehearsed argument on that point. But you mustn't get me mounted on that hobby-horse either. He's unmarried?

Cressida He's a widower. He married an Irish woman. Maureen, her name was. They were not happy. They both drank rather too much.

Uncomfortable silence.

Julian She used to beat him. He was a battered husband –

Cressida Jules, is that really relevant?

Julian Who knows? He never complained. And as far as I know he never hit back, though I often wished he had. Yet, my father-in-law liked her.

Cressida Daddy was a hopeless judge when it came to people. He only ever saw the good in them.

Julian laughs.   wouldn't that work against his support of Romka?

Julian She says that because he only ever saw the good in me. Anyway, one night, about three years ago, Maureen had a heart attack, they'd probably been fighting. But she recovered, decided to convalesce in Ireland and died there. The odd thing is, I believe Romka misses her. Cressy was saying that just the other day.

Marian consults her notes.

Marian Have you ever heard Mr Kozachenko discuss the war?

Brief silence.

Cressida Not really, have you, Jules?

Julian Don't think so –

Marian Never?

Julian We've heard him bang on about the Communists, haven't we? Stalin and all that. How the Ukraine suffered –

Cressida Suffered terribly –

Julian He lost his whole family, parents, brothers, sisters.

Cressida He hated the Communists.

Marian Nothing about the Nazis?

Cressida No. Jules?

Julian No.

Marian Have you ever heard him mention the Jews?

Cressida and Julian No.

Marian You're sure?

Cressida Certain. It's not a subject – we just don't – never have – it's not part of our – there are no Jews living in our village, for example – *just really not aware of subconscious*

Julian I don't know about Milton, he may be – *attitudes*

Uneasy silence.

31

Marian What sort of things do you talk about with Mr Kozachenko?

Cressida Practical things, day-to-day, ordinary things. Daddy used to talk to him more seriously, I think. They were astonishingly close. Spent hours together. They used to go to Mass every Sunday. Somehow, I can't explain this, but I often thought that Romka was Daddy's channel of grace –

Julian That's a 'Carthlick' concept. A channel of grace –

Cressida Julian's lapsed –

Roman enters, holding the piece of wood with Rosie's name on it.

Julian Talk of the devil – (*Laughs feebly.*) Romka, this is Mrs Stone.

Roman bows. Marian nods. Awkward moment.

Cressida Sit down, Romka, join us –

Marian I'd prefer to see Mr Kozachenko alone, if you don't mind.

Cressida and Julian exchange a look. Then:

Cressida I have to start supper –

Julian I'll do the chickens, Romka –

Roman Mr Julian, this is for grave of Rosie –

Julian takes it from him, shudders.

Julian I'll do it –

A moment's hesitation, then Cressida and Julian go their separate ways. Marian takes from her briefcase a pad, some typewritten notes and a pen.

Marian Please sit.

Roman sits.

Mr Kozachenko, you know why I am here?

Roman You are lawyer. And call me Roman. Or Romka. Everybody call me Romka. Kozachenko is mouthful. My Maureen always say, Kozachenko is mouthful.

Marian I want to assure you that whatever you tell me will be entirely confidential. I will not discuss this conversation with anyone, not even with Mr or Mrs Field. Do you understand?

Roman No problem.

Marian So I am going to ask you not to lie to me –

Roman I never lie. I tell truth always. I am honest man. No lies, not me, never.

Marian Good. Then we understand each other. How old are you, Mr Kozachenko?

Roman Seventy-eight. Seventy-nine this year. December.

Marian You do look amazingly well. And you were born in the Western Ukraine.

Roman Small village. Starivka. Maybe eighty kilometres from Vilivsk. South west.

Marian Have you any idea where these alleged murders took place?

Roman No. He don't say. I don't know what murders. I am not murderer. Is crazy –

Marian (*consulting her notes*) There were many atrocities committed in or near Vilivsk.

Roman Madam, I was farm boy. I don't travel. It's not like here. You stay where you are born. I never been to Vilivsk before war. Vilivsk is big town, to me like the

33

moon or United States of America, I never been there –

Marian Does that mean you went to Vilivsk during the war?

Roman You go where they say. That's war. That's army.

Marian Which army?

Roman First, Red Army. I spit on them. I thank God, Communists are gone now. All the prayers of people for this, answered. I am hating Communism. Anti-Christ, you understand me? I am believer.

She consults her notes again.

Marian In the summer of 1941, the Germans attacked Russia and occupied the Ukraine. The Soviets were forced to withdraw. What happened to you?

Roman I dance in street. I am so happy when Communists go. So happy. I think also Ukraine for Ukrainians, not Russians. Is our land. This is what I think. So, I dance. And when Germans come, I am joyful.

Marian How old were you then?

Roman In '41? I am twenty-three.

Marian Of military age.

Roman Sure. We form our own army. Ukrainian.

Marian Which co-operated with the Germans.

Roman Madam, I am cook in army. That is what I do in army. I cook. I never fire shot. I never seen dead body. I am in kitchen. I am cooking. I am good cook. You ask Cressy, Mr Julian, ask friends who come to dinner here, they like what I cook.

She makes notes.

Marian So you know nothing at all about these allegations mentioned by the Detective Inspector?

Roman Nothing. He say me, he got information. But what information, madam? Murder of eight hundred seventeen Jews? He don't say more. I say him I know nothing about these things. Okay, I know Jews were killed. I know this –

Marian Did you know at the time?

Roman Sure, I know. You cannot help knowing. Jews were murdered. This is true. You can't live then and not know. People who say you they don't know, they lie. We knew. We saw. We saw Jews, they take them away, we never see them again. What we think happen? They go for picnic? Can't find way home? No. We know very well what happens. Many, many Jews we knew. In my village lived Jews. And these Jews disappear. They die. They are murdered. Hundreds. Thousands. Terrible, terrible things are done. By Germans. And Ukrainians. I know this. Certain sure I know this. *Then, then, then,* we know it. I say you, madam, you could not live in those times, in that place and not know. Is impossible.

Marian What was your attitude towards the Jews?

Roman shrugs, cannot find words.

You will have to answer, Mr Kozachenko. I've no doubt the police will ask you the same question.

Roman I am not wanting to insult you, madam. Mr Julian say me you are Jew.

Marian No, I'm not. My husband is but I'm not. I'll repeat the question. What was your attitude towards the Jews before and during the war?

After a moment:

35

Roman Okay. I tell you. I hate Communists. Many Jews Communists. Many Jews NKVD, secret police, Stalin people all Jews. Jews have best jobs, in offices always, nice, clean jobs, because, you understand, Jews look after their own. Okay. I say you now, I not like Communists, I not like Jews. To me, the same. But, does not mean I kill Jews, does not mean I am murderer. No. You ask, I tell.

Marian And now?

Roman Now? We are not in Ukraine. I am not that man. I am not that Ukrainian. Okay, I speak bad English, funny accent, Major Leonard he say me, 'Romka, you speak Mau-Mau.' But now, I am British subject. I am different man.

Marian And you are saying that you took no part in any action involving the murder of Jews in 1941?

Roman Never, never, never. I went to priest. Village priest. I remember him like yesterday. Father Alexei. I ask him, please Father, what to do? Evil, I say him, evil is in our land, our village, everywhere, evil. You can smell, you can taste, like sulphur, you know the smell sulphur? You taste and smell sulphur day, night, in the nose, in the mouth. Your eyes water with sulphur. This is what it is like to live then, to live there. I say him, Father Alexei, I am Christian, I say him I cannot live here with these things, with this sulphur, with this terrible evil. I must go. Where, he ask? Where you go? Father Alexei, you understand, he ask where I will go? What answer? No answer. Where I can go? War everywhere. Germans, Russians, Poles, everywhere. War. He say me, Romka, we are all damned. You understand? Damned. This from priest. We are all damned. I remember. I cannot take breath. I have shock like lightning is to strike me. All damned. I remember also tears, tears from that priest, good man, Father Alexei, tears run down cheeks. Because, he say me, we are

36

caught in Devil's trap, Romka. He shout loud, damned. I not understand then. But now, now, I understand.

The light is beginning to fade.

Marian May I see the receipt the Inspector gave you?

Roman hands over the receipt.

What were these photographs. Eight photographs?

Roman Old. From army. With chums.

Marian (*amused*) Chums.

Roman Sure. Catering. Cooks, kitchen help, stewards, they serve officers. Sure. Nothing. No problem.

Marian Have you any idea what evidence the police have?

Roman This is more than fifty years. What can be evidence?

Marian I'm asking you.

Roman Is impossible I know. What evidence, what?

Marian And witnesses?

Roman The same. How can there be witnesses? Witness what? I kill no one. And these witnesses, old men now, like me, all old men. They got such good memories? Fifty years more ago? They remember who, what, where? If they remember me, they remember wrong.

Julian re-enters and hurries into the house. Marian waits for him to go.

Marian You know that members of the War Crimes squad, from Scotland Yard, visited the Ukraine and took statements from a great many people. Do you have any idea who these people might be?

Roman Is impossible I know. I come here to England. I
have no one more in Ukraine. Two brothers, one sister, all
older than me, all dead. Another sister, Larisa, the baby,
for me, favourite, lost. Disappear. No trace. My baby sister, Larisa. This is war. From time I am here I write no
one in Ukraine. No one write me. I am British subject. I
pay taxes. I live quiet, good, make no trouble, you ask
Cressy and Mr Julian. Major Leonard and me are friends.
Every Sunday we go to Mass together. Also his wife, Jane.
I am with her when she die. I carry Major into room and
together with priest, who give Last Rites, Father Vickers,
we pray, all three. And when Major die, I am with him
also, I hold his hand. Fine English gentleman. Yes, I say
you, this is my country now. Here. Great Britain. Good,
just, fair. British justice, top in world. This I believe. This I
trust. And in God I trust. I am loyal subject of Queen
Elizabeth. *—› sounds like he's reciting something*

Brief silence.

Madam, believe me, I am innocent man. I did not kill
Jews. I did not kill anyone. They have wrong man. They
make these mistakes before. I am not murderer. I am not
guilty.

*Silence. It is almost dark now. The lights fade to black-
out.*

*So Anti-semetic at the time
possible change of opinion now
no evidence of murderous impulses*

38

Act Two

An interview room, Scotland Yard. Some weeks later, just after 10 a.m.

Washbourne and Mather sit one side of a table with files, papers; Roman and Marian the other. She, too, keeps notes.

A microphone and tape recorder between them.

Washbourne The time is 10.07 a.m. Mr Kozachenko, if at any time during the interview, you feel in need of refreshment, or want to go to the toilet, or if you are feeling unwell, please say so and we will take a break. (*Consults his notes.*) Mr Kozachenko, since we are satisfied that you entered the United Kingdom legally in February, 1947, and since your naturalization papers and your passport are both in order, I want to begin by asking you about your time spent in detention near Rimini beginning in April, 1945. You were taken prisoner by Allied forces in Austria, is that right?

Roman Yes.

Washbourne And then transferred to a prisoner-of-war camp in Rimini.

Roman Near Rimini. Yes.

Washbourne The majority of Ukrainians who were confined in Rimini were members of the Galicia SS Division, eight thousand of them. Did that include you?

Roman I was in Rimini, yes.

Mather Were you a member of the Galicia SS Division?

Roman Yes. I was cook. For one unit.

Washbourne I shall return to the Galicia SS Division but I want to ask you about something else. The peace treaty between the Allies and the Axis powers contained provisions that all citizens of Allied countries, including, of course, the former Soviet Union, were to be repatriated to their countries of origin. But the British government was reluctant to return Ukrainians to the Soviet Union. They were allowed, therefore, to enter the United Kingdom. Tell me how that happened.

Roman How I get to U.K.?

Washbourne Yes.

Roman I don't remember exactly. Long time now. Fifty years, more, I don't remember –

Washbourne Let me see if I can help you. Britain was suffering from a labour shortage. Do you remember any organizations who were recruiting Ukrainians and others for work in the United Kingdom?

Roman No.

Mather Do you remember being approached by an organization known as the European Voluntary Workers scheme, also known as EVW or by its code name, 'Westward Ho!'?

Roman No.

Washbourne So there must have been another route.

Roman I not remember.

Washbourne But do you remember being asked questions by British Intelligence officers?

Roman Sure, all the time, questions, questions. But British have problems. Many, many prisoners, eight thousand, you say. Very few British for asking questions. They call it screening. This I remember.

Washbourne Is that how you met Major Leonard?

Roman Could be.

Washbourne Don't you remember Major Leonard being one of the officers who screened prisoners?

Roman Sure, but you ask how we meet. This is what I don't remember. Sure, he ask me questions –

Washbourne Well, isn't it a fact that Major Leonard was particularly interested in any information you could give him about Soviet military personnel, weaponry, intelligence matters of various kinds –?

Roman He ask everybody the same –

Washbourne I'm not interested in everybody, Mr Kozachenko, I'm interested in you. Isn't it a fact that, after you were first questioned by Allied intelligence, you gained the impression that you wouldn't be allowed into the United Kingdom?

Roman No, this I don't remember –

Washbourne And isn't it also a fact that the reason you wouldn't be allowed into the United Kingdom was because evidence existed that you had partaken in atrocities concerning the Jewish population in the Western Ukraine?

Roman No, no, this is not right, no evidence, I no take part in nothing, is not possible.

Washbourne Wasn't it then that you approached Major Leonard, who had been one of your interrogators, and offered him information concerning the Soviet military in the hope that this would gain you entry in the United

Kingdom? And the Major said he would see what he could do.

Roman What information? I am cook. What information I give Major Leonard? How to make halushky, varenyky, pampushky? What information has cook?

Marian puts her hand on his arm, restraining him gently.

Washbourne Well, I have a file here, taken during our search, a file kept by Major Leonard at the time, marked 'R. K.' which contains notes of various conversations that he had with you.

Marian Does he mention evidence of atrocities?

Washbourne No. But he does say that Mr Kozachenko feared there would be difficulties about him entering the U.K. and we know that the only reason certain Ukrainian prisoners experienced such difficulties was because they could be connected to atrocities committed during the war. How do you answer that, Mr Kozachenko?

Roman I talk to Major Leonard. This is fact. We become friends. This is fact. He is sick man. Bad leg. Much pain to walk. I help him. He is decent man. He is only British officer who come to Mass with prisoners. Only one. He is good man. After Mass, many times, we walk, I push him in wheelchair. He like me. He say me, Romka, I look after you. This is what he say me. I offer nothing.

Mather Then you claim that the notes kept by Major Leonard at the time are incorrect?

Marian Since he hasn't seen the notes, I don't think my client can be asked to comment.

Washbourne But this is a photograph of you and Major Leonard taken at the time, isn't it? I am showing Mr Kozachenko a photograph removed from Major

Leonard's album, numbered 'LA 4'. There is a British officer in a wheelchair and a soldier, wearing the uniform and
insignia of the Galician SS, is standing behind him.

*He shows Roman a photograph. Roman puts on his
glasses.*

Roman Yes! I have not seen this for many years. Yes.
That's me, that's Major Leonard.

Washbourne reviews his notes.

Washbourne The Galicia SS Division –

Roman We fight Russians, nothing else. Germans make
this division to fight Russians. We lose many, many men.
Many friends die.

Washbourne I understand. The division was formed in
the spring of 1943. It was a volunteer force, is that right?

Roman This is right.

Washbourne And you volunteered?

Roman I am born Ukrainian. You know what Stalin do
to Ukraine? You know what is kulak? My father was
kulak. He is owner of land, small, nothing, market garden
maximum, but, *his*. He owns, you understand? His land.
Stalin say no, this is wrong. No one owns nothing. Only
state owns. Kulaks say no. Resist. What Stalin do? He
make famine in Ukraine. He starve Ukraine. He kill, he
send to Siberia, kulaks, peasants, intelligentsia. All. And
Catholics, yes, all religious he hates. He himself was once
to be priest. He kills priests. Nobody know how many
people he kill, send to Siberia. Thousands, many thousands. My father is one. Two older brothers and sister,
also. My mother she die. Only me and baby sister, Larisa,
we are left. Yes. When Germans come we sing, we dance,
we are joyful. When Germans say we make division to

43

fight Communists, I say, please, I wish to be one.

Mather This was in 1943, yes?

Roman I don't remember –

Washbourne Your pay book has you joining the SS Galicia Division in August 1943.

Brief silence.

According to our figures, eighty thousand Ukrainians registered for the Galicia SS Division, but only nineteen thousand were enlisted. Do you have any idea how the selection was made?

Roman How I know such things? This Germans decide.

Washbourne Isn't it a fact that only those of you were enlisted who had previously been members of the police or members of the Ukrainian militia, the *miliz*, another volunteer force, that had been formed in 1941?

Roman Could be. I don't know.

Washbourne You see, my point is, Mr Kozachenko, that the Germans only recruited Ukrainians who had, as it were, previous experience in the military or police. Does that ring a bell?

Roman Is possible.

Washbourne And you had volunteered for the Ukrainian *miliz* in 1941, hadn't you?

Roman Sure. As cook.

Washbourne Tell me about the militia, the *miliz*.

Roman You got to understand history.

No response.

Hitler, Stalin make treaty, yes? Then, Hitler he attack

44

Stalin. No problem. Then, oh, then, Stalin, before he must go from Ukraine, he kill more Ukrainians, kill, send away, oh my God, how many, how many? But Stalin is gone and now we think we are free. So we make Ukrainian *miliz*. Then, Germans come. And we are friends with Germans because we both hate Stalin.

Washbourne And Jews.

No response.

What was your attitude to the Jews, at that time, Mr Kozachenko?

Roman I tell Mrs Stone. I tell you. Jews and Communists are same to me.

Washbourne You hated the Jews.

Roman Hated, no. I did not like.

Washbourne nods to Mather.

Mather Mr Kozachenko, you may remember that we took some photographs from your rooms, too. We're interested in this one in particular. I am showing Mr Kozachenko a photograph marked 'RK 3'. It's a group of ten soldiers, all in the uniforms of the Ukrainian *miliz*. On the back of the photograph, in faded pencil, is a date, 1941. (*He shows him a photograph.*) Which one are you?

Roman (*pointing*) This one.

Mather Mr Kozachenko has identified himself as standing third from the left. Of course, we know that's you when young, don't we, because we have the photograph of you and Major Leonard taken together in 1945? You hadn't changed much. Lost a bit of weight, but that's all. Can you identify any of your colleagues on this photograph?

45

Roman Colleagues?

Marian Chums.

Roman Fifty years. Difficult. Ah. This boy, his name was also Romka.

A flick between Washbourne and Mather.

Yes, I am sure, because they call me Romka One and this boy, Romka Two. Roman is common name in Ukraine.

Mather Mr Kozachenko has identified a man, second from the left, in the photograph numbered 'RK 3'. Any other names? Look carefully. Think about it.

Roman Is difficult for me. This photograph taken when?

Mather It says on the back 1941. And you're wearing the uniform and insignia of the *miliz*. So it must be '41.

Roman We are talking more than fifty years past. Is difficult. I am old. Memory comes, goes.

Mather What about this man, seated in the centre? I am indicating a man on the same photograph. He is the only one seated.

Roman Ah, yes, sergeant. Tough guy. His name? My God. No. He was with us very small time. No.

Mather Do you remember what his duties were?

Roman Sergeant? He see we do what we're told. He is sergeant.

Mather No cooking?

Roman I don't remember. No. Not. No. No cooking. Sergeants? No.

Mather Does the name Fedorenko mean anything to you?

46

Roman (*uneasy*) Fedorenko, Fedorenko, is common name, Fedorenko. In this unit?

Washbourne And the name Demidenko?

Roman Demidenko. I remember girl, Demidenko. Can't remember first name. Friend from my sister. Live in same house. Yes, I remember Demidenko. She is alive now?

No response. Washbourne and Mather consult their notes.

Marian Inspector, you have been questioning my client for some time and, so far, you have not linked him to any crime or, indeed, to any incident whatsoever which might be characterized as criminal.

Washbourne We will be dealing with that shortly. But what we are attempting to do now, Mrs Stone, is to establish links in the chain which confirms that Mr Kozachenko was in such-and-such a place at such-and-such a time –

Marian What place, what time?

Washbourne That also, I assure you, will become clear. Now, Mr Kozachenko, the name Fedorenko –

Roman I would like toilet, please.

Brief, awkward pause.

Washbourne Of course. The interview is being suspended at 10.24 a.m. (*He switches off the recorder.*) Perhaps you would like a break, too, Mrs Stone?

Marian Thank you.

Washbourne Just knock when you want to come back in.

Roman and Marian leave.

How did we do?

Mather Well.

Washbourne I thought Fedorenko shook him a little.

Mather Yes –

Washbourne But he admitted to remembering Demidenko.

Brief silence.

But what about this other little bugger called Romka, Romka Two. Who's he?

Mather I don't know – (*Pages through a file.*) Nothing on him. No mention of a second Romka anywhere. He's not on any of the duty rosters. Not on the Order of the Day.

Washbourne Perhaps Sunshine invented him.

Mather Bloody clever if he did, guv.

They study their notes.

Washbourne Could undermine the first cohort witness.

Mather But the second one's still safe. No trouble with her. No trouble whatsoever.

Washbourne We'll have to check this Romka Two with Kiev. Send a fax when we break for lunch.

Mather Right. But it'll take them a year to answer.

Washbourne Did I miss anything?

Mather I don't think so.

Washbourne When Sunshine comes back I'll get to the crime –

Mather (*imitating Roman*) No, I not remember, I cook, I make baked beans on toast –

They laugh. definitely no innocent until proven guilty here

48

The brief's good.

Washbourne Yeah, knows when to talk and when to keep shtum.

A knock on the door.

Okay. I'll ask Sunshine about the crime. You do the cohort witness.

Mather Right.

Washbourne (*calling*) Yes?

Marian returns.

Mather Tea, coffee, Mrs Stone?

Marian No, thank you. (*She sits.*) Do you have a big staff, Inspector?

Washbourne Six of us. A couple of historians, admin.

She studies Washbourne.

Marian Inspector, may I ask you a question?

Washbourne By all means.

Marian Have you come under any pressure because of working for the War Crimes squad?

Washbourne Mr Field gave me some stick when we served the search warrant. Thought I'd be better employed investigating the theft of his car radio from Chester Row. But I'm used to that.

Marian No, I meant moral pressure.

Washbourne Moral pressure. Oh, dear. From whom?

Marian Colleagues, friends, family. People who say it's wrong to rake up the past, to pursue old men, that sort of thing.

Washbourne Yes. Once or twice.

Marian And how do you answer them?

Washbourne I say if the suspect is guilty, then he's had fifty years longer on this planet than the people he killed.

Silence. A knock on the door.

Mather Yes?

Roman returns.

Washbourne All right, Mr Kozachenko?

Roman Thank you,

Mather Tea, coffee?

Roman No, thank you.

Washbourne (*switching on recording*) This interview of Mr Roman Kozachenko is being resumed at 10.38 a.m. Officers present, D. I. Washbourne and D. C. Mather and Mr Kozachenko's solicitor, Mrs Marian Stone. Mr Kozachenko, you were born in Starivka, is that correct?

Roman Correct. Second of December, 1917.

Washbourne So you know, of course, the neighbouring village of Mikolja and the town of Kovlici. Forgive my pronunciation –

Roman Mikolja and Kovlici, I know, sure.

Washbourne And you had occasion to visit those places in late August, 1941?

Roman laughs.

Roman I don't remember. Is not possible I remember. I go many times to these places –

Washbourne Let's see if I can help you. We have duty rosters and an Order of the Day for your particular unit which was stationed in Vilivsk. And those documents show that you were ordered to your home village of Starivka, to Mikolja and Kovlici over a period of three days, 29th, 30th, 31st August, 1941.

Roman Unit, maybe, not cooks. We stay in Vilivsk.

Washbourne Your name is on the duty roster. And on this Order of the Day. I am showing Mr Kozachenko an exhibit marked 'Kiev Archive 82'.

Hands Roman a paper; Roman puts on his glasses and reads.

Can you read the signature?

Roman Fedorenko.

Washbourne And doesn't it say – this is a rough translation – 'The following will report for action in Starivka, Mikolja and Kovlici'?

Roman Yes –

Washbourne And is it dated 27th August, 1941?

Roman Yes –

Washbourne And isn't your name on that list, there, R. I. Kozachenko?

Roman Yes, but does not mean I go with unit. It means I am on duty, yes, to cook for unit. We stay in Vilivsk. And, look! Here is Romka Two. R. G. Kvitka. Now, I remember –

Washbourne But, according to the records in Kiev, we have this man, Kvitka, as Ruslan Grigorovich –

Roman No, no, he is Roman, like me, I remember, *Roman* Grigorovich, I remember. Sure, man with same

51

name, I remember. He is Romka Two. Educated boy. Good family. Mother, Russian. I remember.

Washbourne Put that aside for a moment. You say you remained in Vilivsk. The Order says you are to leave Vilivsk for three days, and names specific places in which your unit is to take action. Yes?

Roman Yes.

Washbourne My question is, why, as you claim, would you remain in Vilivsk, as a cook, when your unit has been ordered away? Who would you cook for? What would be the point of you remaining in Vilivsk when your unit isn't there?

Roman I say you, Inspector, cooks did not always go with unit. This happens many, many times. This was Ukrainian *miliz*, not German army. Rosters! Our officers, they are thinking they are German High Command. Rosters, orders, even give us menus. This you must cook. We cook what we have. Rosters! Orders! Is crazy.

Washbourne So, what you are saying is that you were in Vilivsk on the last three days of August, 1941 –

Roman I not remember the dates –

Washbourne Then how do you remember not being with your unit?

Roman Because I *never* go with unit. This I remember. Never. Where, how, what would I cook? We have kitchen in Vilivsk, in army camp. There I cook. Where I cook in these places? Go into private house? Cook? Is not possible.

Washbourne Well, Mr Kozachenko, we have witnesses who say you were with the unit during that period, that you were in Starivka, Mikolja and Kovlici on the days in question.

Uneasy silence. Washbourne nods to Mather.

Mather I am going to read to you from a transcript of evidence taken in Vilivsk on 12th May last year. (*Hands a copy to Marian.*) The witness's name is Nikolai Mihailovich Fedorenko, known as Nikita Fedorenko. He was questioned by me through an interpreter. I did not, at first, tell him the purpose of the interview. We simply said we were making general enquiries. Question: Please state your name.

Light grows on Nikita Fedorenko, seated, aged 82, fierce, a chain-smoker.

(*continuing*) My name is Nikolai Mihailovich Fedorenko. But they call me Nikita. It is short for Nikolai. Question: Please state your age. Answer: I am eighty-two years old and I smoke like a chimney. And the young girls still love me. And I love them. Not bad, eh?

Nikita (*simultaneously*) And the young girls still love me. And I love them. Not bad, eh?

Mather What is your occupation?

Nikita Jail-bird. (*He laughs.*)

Mather Why do you say that?

Nikita Because I have spent thirty years in prison. 1946 to 1976. Soviet bastards put me there. Siberia. Gulag.

Mather What was your crime?

Nikita I fought with Germans against Communists. I killed Communists. Many.

Mather And Jews?

Nikita Sure. I'm lucky to be alive. They wanted to shoot me. But I had friends, Ukrainian friends in high places, who did not think I had done such terrible things. They looked after me.

Mather You served, didn't you, in the Ukrainian *miliz* which was formed in 1941.

Nikita Correct. I was a sergeant.

Mather Please look at this photograph. It comes from the archive in Kiev.

Washbourne (*to Roman and Marian*) This was a mug shot, taken in or about 1941, we think for an identity card.

Nikita I don't need glasses either. Eighty-two. They don't breed them like me any more. Unfortunately. (*Looks at the photograph.*) My God! Romka! Little Romka. I don't remember his other name. Where's he now?

Mather Living in England.

Nikita Is that a fact? Romka. Useful man. Could do anything.

Mather Was he a member of your unit?

Nikita Sure.

Mather What were his duties?

Nikita Same as everybody else. He was a soldier –

Roman No, no, he's wrong, I was cook, he remembers wrong –

Mather Now would you look at this? It's an Order of the Day, also from the Kiev Archive. Is that your signature?

Nikita Hey! Where d'you get these things? These are historical documents. They're probably valuable. Yes, that's my signature, all right.

Mather You see on that list, in your handwriting, the name, R. I. Kozachenko?

Nikita Kozachenko, that's him. Romka.

Mather And you see from that Order, that you instructed your unit to prepare for action in Starivka, Mikolja and Kovlici on 28th, 29th and 30th August.

Nikita Yes –

Mather Who had given you orders? The Germans?

Nikita No, we didn't need orders. We were volunteers. We just knew what had to be done.

Mather And what had to be done?

Nikita The usual. (*He winks and draws a forefinger across his throat.*)

Mather The witness winked and drew his forefinger across his throat. Question: What d'you mean by the usual?

Nikita They call it ethnic cleansing now. But just remember, we were the pioneers.

Mather Was this R. I. Kozachenko with you on those days?

Nikita Why are you so interested in Romka? He's still alive, you say. A-ha! Yes, yes, yes, I think I understand. Well, if I've done time, why shouldn't he? (*He chuckles.*)

Mather Just tell me what happened.

Nikita I don't remember everything exactly. You know, one action was very like another. But I remember Mikolja because there must have been about four or five hundred.

Mather Four or five hundred?

Nikita Jews.

Mather Tell me.

Nikita We went from Vilivsk in a truck. The whole unit. About ten of us. We had machine guns, rifles, pistols. And also spades, picks, forks. And sacks of lime. We had many sacks of lime. Terrible smell, you know. Makes your eyes water. We headed for Mikolja. We sang. We always sang. The local police were in on it, too. They had advance warning and orders to round up the Jews. The Jews were told that we were going to take a census. Usually, by the time we arrived, the Jews were already assembled. In Mikolja, you can check this, I'm not absolutely sure, but I think they'd been taken to a wood on the outskirts of the town. Or was that somewhere else? Anyway, what's it matter? It was a wood or a clearing, something like that. The police took the census, they really did. But I seem to remember four hundred give or take a Jew. So. We made them dig a pit. By then they knew what we were really up to so we started to assemble our machine guns.

Mather Men, women and children?

Nikita Yes. All the Jews. Later, the Germans preferred to deal only with the adults. They left the children to us. We didn't ask them to undress or anything. The Germans always did that but we didn't.

Mather What happened after you assembled your machine guns?

Nikita We waited for them to finish digging the pit and then we opened fire.

Mather And Romka Kozachenko was with you?

Roman No! No! Not me, not me –

Nikita Sure he was with me, he was right beside me –

Roman No, no, is lie, is wrong –

Marian tries to restrain him.

56

Nikita – on a machine gun. Others preferred rifles, pick off one at a time, but Romka and me, we preferred machine guns. More efficient.

Roman Is not me, is other Romka, Romka Two, it is not me! He lies! He remembers wrong!

Washbourne Quietly, Mr Kozachenko, let's hear it through –

Mather And afterwards?

Nikita Well. Let's see. Those who hadn't fallen into the pit, we shoved in ourselves. Of course, we made sure no one was breathing. Then we sprinkled them with the lime and covered them up. I think they've put up a memorial there. You should check. And when it was all done, depending on the time, we'd either eat or we'd go on to other places. And we weren't the only unit at work. In Kiev, my God, they were busier than we were.

Mather If necessary, would you be willing to travel to the United Kingdom to give this evidence in court?

Nikita Sure, I've never been there. I hear the girls there are pretty – (*He chuckles.*)

Mather Is there anything you want to add?

Nikita Yes, there is. Do you know how many Jews are back here now, in the Western Ukraine? Six thousand! Yes. I tell you what. (*The light begins to fade on him.*) Give me a machine gun and I'd do it all over again. I don't mind saying that in your court either. Give me Romka beside me and we shoot the lot. Good man, Romka. Good worker.

Mather (*simultaneously*) I don't mind saying that in your court either. Give me Romka beside me and we shoot the lot. Good man, Romka. Good worker.

Silence.

Washbourne The census figures reveal that over those three days eight hundred and seventeen Jews were murdered. Four hundred and thirty-six in Mikolja, one hundred and forty-three in Kovlici and two hundred and thirty-eight in Starivka. There is a memorial in Mikolja but there are no names of the victims.

> *Silence. All Roman does is shake his head from side to side in denial.*
>> *The lights fade to blackout.*

The sound of music from The Magic Flute. *Lights on.*
> *Julian sitting alone, drinking wine. He replenishes his glass often. About 9 p.m. Dark. The only light comes from the house. The music is also coming from the house. He is listening to 'Bei Männern, welche Liebe fühlen', which gives way to 'Zum Ziele führt dich diese Bahn'. The music plays throughout the scene.*
> *After some moments, Cressida enters.*

Cressida That was Marian Stone. She's only just left him.

Julian Where are they?

Cressida She put him in a hotel near Victoria Station. She says he's utterly exhausted.

Julian How did she say it went?

Cressida Gruelling. She sounded exhausted herself. But she says she doesn't think the identification evidence will hold up. There was, apparently, another man called Romka involved. The police are checking. They want them back tomorrow morning. But she said she's fearful for tomorrow. She thinks the Inspector has something up his sleeve.

Brief silence.

I wish this weather would break.

Julian Rain's forecast.

Brief silence.

I hope it's a cheap hotel.

Cressida God, Julian, you're crass.

Julian Never mind crass, you know what this is going to cost?

Cressida What's it matter what it's going to cost?

Julian What's it matter? What's it matter? It matters because I've got to bloody well pay for it, and it could all be for nothing, wasted, down the plug hole –

Cressida (*overlapping*) What about Legal Aid?

Julian What Legal Aid, what Legal Aid, I'm his bloody legal aid –?

Cressida He can apply for Legal Aid –

Julian And if he's not eligible –

Cressida (*overlapping*) Why shouldn't he be eligible –?

Julian (*continuing*) – for one reason or another –

Cressida (*overlapping*) Marian Stone said he'd be eligible –

Julian Marian Stone, Marian Stone, Marian Stone, good, if she says he's eligible then he's eligible, good, good –

Cressida You think he's guilty, don't you –?

Julian I don't know what to think, what do you think?

Cressida I don't know what to think either –

Julian That makes a change –

Cressida Talk to me, Julian, I'm holding on by a thread –
I haven't slept – the heat – the anxiety – I can't – I don't –
for God's sake –

Julian Hasn't Adult Education got an answer to this?
Doesn't Gender Studies give us a clue? If it was a woman
who'd been accused, then you'd probably come to the
immediate conclusion that she was innocent. But because
it's a man, you're in difficulty, isn't that the game? Isn't
that where Gender Studies have led you?

Cressida Don't be so cruel, Julian, just shut up. Shut up!

Silence. She pours herself a drink.

I wish I liked Marian Stone.

Julian I like her. Very attractive. What your father would
have called a good sport. She's bright, you know. Rodney
told me she took a First in Philosophy. She gives lectures –

Cressida You're telling me –

Julian – she's published essays. Married to Gerald Stone.
Obviously knows what she's doing. Although I'm not sure
about kick-boxing. Seemed a bit extreme.

Cressida I'm relieved she's not Jewish. That would have
been truly awkward and embarrassing.

Julian Next best thing. (*He laughs to himself.*)

Cressida She's so holier-than-thou. So certain. So con-
trolled. And d'you remember when I said Romka's not
evil, she said don't get me started on my hobby-horse.
What did she mean, I wonder?

Julian No idea, but here's a clue to her. She doesn't like
opera.

Cressida Oh, Julian, stop being so trivial –

yes, please

60

Julian Prefers the theatre. Think about it.

Cressida Can't you take anything seriously?

Julian Certainly not. I'm English. Holding on to identity in uncertain times

Cressida Julian, do shut up!

Silence.

Julian I keep remembering something your father said to me. Just before he died. I was going to tell the Inspector when he interviewed us, but I decided against it. Thought it best to show a united front. Loyalty's the name of the game.

Cressida What did Daddy say? Daddy adored Romka, what did he say?

Julian Out of the blue, apropos of nothing, I'll never forget it, he said, 'Odd about Romka. You'd think he'd show signs of remorse.' 'About what?' I said. And your Dad turned to look at me, and he worked his lips, you remember the way he used to work his lips when he was flustered or about to flare, and I thought then that he'd let something slip. He said, 'Nothing, nothing. Remorse about fighting for the Nazis, that's all.'

Cressida If he said that, that's what he meant.

Julian No. He was covering something. I know it.

Cressida Rubbish. → blind

Silence. Julian drinks.

Julian Just suppose I'm right. Just suppose he is guilty. You'd think that he would suffer from remorse and show it. Distress. Anguish. Something.

Cressida Well, he doesn't, does he?

Julian No, but I've always thought that when he and

Maureen had a spat, and he'd appear the next morning with a black eye or a cut across his lip, he liked it, wanted it, needed it –

Cressida No pop psychology, please, Julian –

Julian I think he wanted to be punished –

Cressida Oh God, yes, wanted to be punished, now I know why you're in derivatives –

Julian Guilt is a hard thing to bear, Cressida –

Cressida How would you know? What do you know about guilt?

Cressida sits. The light has almost gone. They drink their wine.

Julian Don't look at me, Cressy.

She looks at him.

No, no, don't, turn away, please don't look at me.

She looks away; he finds courage.

I had an affair. Two years ago. Sybilla, her name was. It lasted about nine months. I was in love with her. I was besotted. Obsessed. I couldn't think of anything else. And then, gradually, I couldn't bear the lying any more. Lying to you. I couldn't bear it. And because I'm a card-carrying coward I delayed breaking it off time and time again. I'd get the chance to say, 'This must stop' but I couldn't do it. And then you told me you thought you were pregnant. I finally found courage. I broke it off. And I felt a great lightness. And I went into the Oratory and confessed. And for several months I was free of it but the guilt returned, I don't know why. I can't say it's with me all the time, but often, like an open sore that only your forgiveness can heal.

Brief silence. Cressida stands.

Cressida I knew all about that months ago. She was Swedish. She lived in Chester Row.

Julian You knew? You knew? How did you know?

Cressida You told me. Oh wow.

> *She goes into the house. Julian watches her. The music plays.*
> *The lights fade to blackout.*

Lights on.
> *The interview room at Scotland Yard. The following morning. A TV monitor has been added.*
> *They sit as before: Washbourne and Mather across from Roman and Marian.*

Washbourne Am I to understand, Mrs Stone, that your client wants to make a statement?

Marian Not formally, no. But he does want to say something.

Washbourne Yes, Mr Kozachenko?

> *Roman hesitates.*

Marian Go on.

Roman Sir. All day yesterday you question me. I answer. I tell truth. You have this witness, Fedorenko. More old than me. This is terrible man, Fedorenko. You read me what he say. 'Give me machine gun,' he say, 'I do it again.' This is evil man, evil, evil man. But I have no chance to say him, 'Fedorenko, you lie, Fedorenko, you have wrong man, Fedorenko, you remember wrong.' (*He waits; no response.*) When we stop yesterday, I am tired, cannot think, don't know what, where, why. I am old man. This you must understand. (*Again he waits; again no response.*) But now, today, I am fresh and I wish to question this Fedorenko. He is wrong. All the time wrong. I must say him, 'I am not that Romka –'

Mather But he identified you from the photograph, sir –

Roman He make mistake! He forget Romka Two. My God! He has eighty-two years, his memory is perfect? Impossible. I say you, sir, please, this is not right. I must question this Fedorenko. I must say him, 'You not remember Romka Two?' His word, my word, this is all you got. This is not right.

Marian What my client is asking, Inspector, is will he have the opportunity, should you bring charges, to challenge this witness?

Washbourne After our investigations are complete and, if we see fit, we will pass our findings on to the Crown Prosecution Service and the Attorney General who will then decide whether or not your client has a case to answer. If he does, then you will have every opportunity to question witnesses. In the meantime, we have to test all the evidence we've been able to gather. And that's what we're doing now.

Brief pause.

Mr Kozachenko, when we left off yesterday, we were discussing the events in your home village of Starivka. You flatly denied that you had taken part in any action against the two hundred and thirty-eight Jews who lived there. Is that right?

Roman Right. I knew those families. Good people. Not like others. Poor. Like us. Is not possible I harm them. This is more Fedorenko lies.

Washbourne waits to see if he will continue. Then:

64

Washbourne We have another witness whose testimony we'd like you to hear and then comment on. This was recorded on video in Jerusalem earlier this year. I myself questioned the witness through an interpreter. I told her we were interested in any information she could give us about Roman Kozachenko. Now, if you'd just look at the screen –

He turns on the video player. Light grows on a nun, Sister Sophia, aged 75, a woman of great stillness and dignity.

Please state your name and age.

Roman puts on his glasses, leans forward to be closer to the screen.

Sister Sophia My name is Sister Sophia. I am seventy-five years old. I live here in Jerusalem, in the House of my order and have done for the past forty-eight years.

Washbourne Sophia is your religious name.

Sister Sophia Yes –

Washbourne What was your name originally?

Sister Sophia I was born Natalia Borisovna Demidenko.

A sharp, short grunt from Roman.

I was born in Starivka, a village some kilometres south of Vilivsk, in the Ukraine, on 3rd of June 1921.

Washbourne I want to question you about events that took place in your village on the 31st of August, 1941.

Sister Sophia I can't possibly remember something that happened on a specific date so long ago.

Washbourne We believe it was on that date that the Jews of Starivka were murdered.

He waits; she is still and silent for some moments.

You remember that day now? The 31st of August, 1941?

Sister Sophia If that is the day of the massacre, of course. I shall never forget it. I have offered more prayers for that day than for any other event in my life, secular or religious. And this is about Romka Kozachenko?

Washbourne Yes. What do you remember?

Sister Sophia There were several Jewish families living at that time in Starivka. Many had relatives with them at that time, people who were trying to find a safe haven, because, as I'm sure you know, the Jews were being persecuted on an unendurable scale. I cannot be sure but my guess is that there were more than two hundred Jews, perhaps as many as two hundred and fifty in Starivka on that day.

Washbourne Where were you?

Sister Sophia I was in our room in a house we shared with other orphans. Because, you see, the Communists had driven many people away, and killed many more, especially the kulaks, and my father was a kulak, a small land-owner, so there were many children without parents. Both my parents were dead. Murdered by the Communists. I shared a small room with another orphan. The room was roughly the same size as the cell I now occupy alone. My room mate was Larisa Ivanovna Kozachenko, Romka's sister.

Another grunt from Roman.

Romka also lived in the house. 1941, you say. I would have been – twenty. I worked in the fields for the local state farm. But on that day, early in the morning, I think, the foreman came to tell us that we must not go to work that day and that we must keep indoors. I remember – it's odd

66

what you remember – I remember it was unusually hot.

Washbourne Was Larisa Kozachenko with you on that day?

Sister Sophia Yes.

Washbourne And her brother?

Sister Sophia No. He had joined the Ukrainian militia.

Washbourne What happened after you were told not to go to work and to stay indoors?

Sister Sophia Larisa and I wondered why such an order had been given. I suppose we speculated, chattered as young girls do, I can't remember in detail but I remember we were together when we heard crying, more than cry-ing, children howling, women wailing. And we looked out of the window and saw the Jews of Starivka and all their relatives being marched towards the woods on the out-skirts of the village by the militia. And that's when Larisa noticed that her brother, Romka, was one of the soldiers, and that he was carrying a rifle –

Roman Cannot be, cannot be – ↱selective memory?

Sister Sophia (*overlapping*) – which he used to push these poor people, to make them walk faster. And the Jewish women were holding their frightened children. They were wailing. And the children were crying. I can hear it now. You don't forget things like that.

Washbourne Can you remember anything else about that scene?

Sister Sophia thinks for a moment.

Sister Sophia Yes. I remember a truck followed the proces-sion. And I'll tell you why I remember. Because something was spilling out of the back, it looked like a white powder which I learned later was lime, and it left a trail all the way to the woods. And I shall never forget that either.

Washbourne What did you do after you'd seen the Jews and the militia?

Sister Sophia I said to Larisa, let's follow them, see what they're going to do. I was a bit of a rebel in those days. But she wouldn't go. She was frightened. I think because she had seen her brother. And because I think we secretly knew what was going to happen. We just knew. There had been rumours and stories and – (*She falls silent.*)

Washbourne So what did you do?

Sister Sophia I slipped out of the house and took a roundabout path to the woods. I hadn't gone very far when I heard machine-guns firing and rifle shots. And screams – screams I shall also never forget as long as I live. And birds screeching. It was such a lovely summer's day. I don't suppose it lasted very long and then, when all was quiet, I continued on my way. I came into a hollow. Carefully, I raised my head to look over the verge. (*She falls silent.*)

Washbourne What did you see?

Sister Sophia I saw the militia sprinkling lime into a large, deep trench. I knew it was lime because I could smell it. I could not see into the trench. But I saw several human hands reaching out of the pit clawing at the earth. And this is the most terrible thing. I saw Larisa's brother, Romka, walking up and down with his rifle and firing.

Roman Is not true, I was not there!

Sister Sophia (*overlapping*) The hands disappeared.

Washbourne Are you sure it was this man, Roman Kozachenko?

Sister Sophia Sure.

Washbourne It's more than fifty years ago.

Sister Sophia It is branded in my memory.

Brief silence.

Washbourne After you saw these things, what did you do?

Sister Sophia I would have run away but while some of the soldiers were covering in the pit, others were in the woods searching for firewood. I was frightened. I knew there would be trouble if I was caught. I hid there and waited until it was dark. When I stood I saw that the militia were preparing their meal. Many of them were drunk. And I saw Romka again.

Washbourne How could you see him if it was already dark?

Sister Sophia Because he was squatting by a fire and his face was illuminated by the glow. He was cooking food and dishing it out. I remember that clearly.

Washbourne Did you go back to your room?

Sister Sophia Yes. And I did a very stupid thing. I told Larisa what I had seen. I had to tell someone. She wouldn't believe me –

Roman Because is not true –

Sister Sophia She started to cry and scream. She threatened to report me. So, I ran to the church, to Father Alexei, the village priest, and confessed. I did that because I didn't want to get Father Alexei into trouble. If I hadn't told him in the confessional, it would have been dangerous for him. But, even so, I had the impression that he already knew. I asked for guidance. He said we must pray.

So I sat at the back of our little church and I prayed. Then something very strange happened. I was on my knees, my head bowed, deep in prayer, when I heard the noise of boots on the stone floor. I looked up and saw there were three young soldiers, members of the militia. One of them was Romka. He went into the confessional. He wasn't in very long when he sort of burst out. That's the only way I can describe it. He burst out. And a moment later, Father Alexei appeared and shouted, 'Damned! You are damned!' The soldiers fled. He ran to the door and shouted into the night, 'Damned!' Then Father Alexei dropped to his knees and prayed. He was in a terrible state. At last, he stood and came to me. He said I must go into hiding. He put me in the back of his cart, covered me in blankets and hay, and drove me to the Convent near Petrovodi, it doesn't exist any more, the Communists destroyed it, and the sisters took me in. Some weeks later, I heard that Father Alexei had been shot by the Germans.

Washbourne When you were praying in the church and the soldiers came in, did they see you?

Sister Sophia I don't know –

Washbourne And when Roman Kozachenko burst out of the confessional, did he see you then?

Sister Sophia I really can't say – I don't think so – I simply can't remember –

Washbourne Do you know what happened to Larisa Kozachenko?

Sister Sophia Only a rumour. I heard she had reported me to the authorities. And they shot her.

A harsh, dry sob from Roman. Guilt or just grief?

Because, you see, she knew too much.

Washbourne How long did you remain in the convent?

Sister Sophia I never left. I entered the order. And after the war, I was sent here, to our house in Jerusalem.

Washbourne Is there anything more you want to tell me?

She considers for a moment.

Sister Sophia Throughout all my religious life, I have been praying for guidance. I have spent long hours in contemplation and I have sought advice from those wiser and more learned than I. I have asked why? Why have the Jews been made to suffer so appallingly? And I have come to this conclusion. It is not because one of their number betrayed Our Lord. It is not because they handed Him over to the Romans, knowing He would be crucified. No. It is because they have rejected Him. They rejected Our Lord Jesus Christ as the Son of God, and do not believe He is the true Messiah. For that, they have been mercilessly persecuted. And if Romka Kozachenko is to be punished for his sins, I will give thanks. Not because I believe justice must be done or that his victims will be revenged or that he deserves to be punished, though I do believe all those things. No, I will give thanks because his suffering will be the only path of his eternal soul to true, everlasting redemption.

The light fades on her. Silence in the interview room. Then, Roman suddenly stands and emits a horrifying cry from the depths of his being, long and agonizing. When the cry is spent, he groans, painful, noisy gasps for breath.   I can't imagine how an actor
                                   would do this.
No one else moves.
The lights fade to blackout.

Lights on.

The terrace of the Field's house. Some weeks later. Noon.
Julian, wearing a suit, is on his mobile, pacing, waiting
for his call to be answered. Cressida, her appearance
neglected, and Roman, wearing his same suit, enter from
the house. Cressida holds Roman's hand.

Julian I'm going to have them moved if it's the last thing I
do – (*into telephone*) Rodney? Julian. Look, we've just
come back from the magistrate's court and – what –?
(*Listens.*) Yes, yes, he got bail, of course, he got bail, I
stood surety, but that's not the point, the point is that the
grubbies are at my gate. (*Listens.*) The grubbies.
Journalists, grubbies, get born, Rodney. About fifty of
them, TV cameras, the bloody lot – (*Listens.*) Never mind
that, my question is, how do we get rid of them?
(*Listens.*) No, they're not in the drive or at the door.
They're outside the gates – (*Listens.*) But that's ridiculous!
They're causing a nuisance, they're making a mess and a
bloody noise. We could hardly drive through, flash bulbs
going, microphones stuck into the car – (*Listens.*) Well,
you're a fat lot of use – (*He clicks off the telephone, puts
it away.*)

Cressida What's he say?

Julian If they're not trespassing – (*He breaks off.*)

Cressida Romka, you should lie down now.

Roman No.

Marian enters from the house.

Cressida (*near to tears*) Please, Romka, don't argue with
me –

Julian Romka, do as you're told for once in your life.

Cressida Julian, please, he's not well. And I'm not in the

72

best of spirits either. So, please let's just – come on, Romka. I'll take you –

She leads Roman away. Silence.

Julian What now?

Marian We instruct counsel.

Julian You're sure he'll get Legal Aid?

Marian Yes.

Silence.

Julian My wife's not very well.

Marian Yes. I was quite shocked when I saw her today. I haven't seen her for some weeks and –

Julian She has nightmares. Every night since –. She hasn't done any of her work. She remembers some things, not others. She remembers wrongly. I want her to see a doctor but will she? No.

Marian It's understandable, don't you think?

Julian What, that she won't see a doctor? (*He paces, then stops, sits.*) I'm surprised they charged him. You said the identification evidence was dodgy, that all the other evidence was circumstantial, yet here we are, he's charged and committed for trial. And the world's media is camped on our doorstep. Terrific.

Marian There's a case to be answered.

Cressida returns.

Cressida He wouldn't go to bed. He's just sitting there, slumped in a chair. (*Silence.*) Oh God, I can't stop crying. (*Silence.*) I thought what happened today was sickening. (*Silence.*) A poor old man in the dock, policemen either side of him, a poor old man charged with crimes he's supposed to have committed fifty-five years ago. It's immoral. It's unjust. It's uncivilized. How can he get a fair trial? We know what a jury will say. They'll say if the police have gone to all this trouble, he must be guilty. Or are we going to have trial by the media? And what evidence do they have? Two old people, as old as he, older, remembering events fifty years ago? How can you trust their memories? I can't trust mine. Romka says he wasn't there. How's he going to prove that? Is he going to find other elderly witnesses who'll give him an alibi? In the end, it'll be his word against theirs and I believe him. He's my friend. And I rate friendship above – I put loyalty to a friend – It's ludicrous! You know what I think it is? I think it's nothing short of retribution. *but for a good reason?*

Marian I suppose all court cases, whether they impose fines or prison sentences are, in one way or another, retribution.

Cressida Don't patronize me. It's revenge. That's all. Old-fashioned, Old Testament revenge. Nothing more. Nothing less. And they should say so. He's seventy-eight, for God's sake. You just have to look at him, he's not going to harm anybody now, if ever he did, you can see, you can see he's not evil.

Marian They were none of them evil.

Cressida And don't preach. For God's sake, don't preach at me –

Marian I'm not preaching –

Cressida Oh yes, you are, I can hear it in your tone, smug, cheerful, pious – *approaching hysterics*

Julian Cressy, calm down –

Cressida I won't calm down, I don't want her preaching at me –

74

Julian Don't talk to her like that, Cressy –

Marian Mrs Field, you can talk to me how you like, I really don't mind. But I will not have you falling into error which, I am sure, is a phrase you understand. My husband and I often have this argument. He also believes in evil. I don't –

Cressida Oh, this is the hobby-horse, is it? Is this what you meant by your hobby-horse?

Marian Entire nations we are told, were manipulated, duped, corrupted by a handful of evil men. I don't accept it and I never have. To believe in evil absolves us of all responsibility –

Cressida You're lecturing me, I don't want to hear, don't lecture me, please, please, I don't want to hear –

Marian (*continuing blithely*) What happened was human, unfortunately and reprehensibly human. Not banal, as some have claimed. But human. Like us. Now, I deplore violence –

Julian Yes, yes, we all deplore violence –

Marian I hope so. I deplore violence, but I know the violence in me. To believe for one moment that the perpetrators were evil instantly lets us off the hook. Think of the numbers murdered, six million Jews, millions of others, just think of the numbers who had to be involved in their destruction. Thousands. Countless thousands. Hundreds of thousands. All of them evil? No. None of them. You are right. Mr Kozachenko is not evil. Nothing about Mr Kozachenko is evil and never was. He is intensely, pathetically human. But he is to be defended and he is to be defended well. Which means I will do my best for him. I will not allow a system, a society in which I enjoy a great deal of freedom, to be accused of betraying in a court of

a robot. but a good point.
what a

law the highest standards of fairness and decency for which it is justly renowned –

Julian Christ, you're complacent. Our beloved system isn't perfect, is it? It makes gigantic cock-ups because judges always believe the police and the police do anything they can to get a conviction.

Marian Nevertheless. The cock-ups have been revealed, decisions reversed. That, too, is part of the system.

Cressida There's only one question –

Julian Cressy, please, calm down, stop crying –

Cressida I can't! (*She subsides for a moment.*)

Julian Well, if you want my theory, I think it's culling.

Marian You think it's what?

Julian Culling. I think we're still in the jungle, crawling in the primeval slime. Yes, I think it's our way of culling the population. Not human at all, but animal, atavistic, primitive impulse. There are too many of us and so we're simply compelled to reduce numbers. That's why it goes on all the time. But that's something we don't want to believe so we put a certain kind of spin on it, and call it genocide and Holocaust and mass murder but all we're doing is culling. We have no choice.

Marian No choice? That's disgusting. That removes the notion of responsibility which is intolerable. And what happened to morality, a sense of right and wrong, that imposes the most dreadful obligation and makes us accountable. It was mass murder, organized on a vast scale. Culling? Balls. I feel like I would like her if she was more concise

Cressida (*still crying; to Marian*) I want my question answered. It's the only question worth asking. Do you believe Romka's guilty?

Marian Belief? What has belief got to do with it? Belief belongs in church. I am here to see that Mr Kozachenko gets a fair trial and that the witnesses are credible. Belief doesn't enter into it.

Cressida Guilty or not, poor old men should not be brought to trial for crimes they're alleged to have committed more than fifty years ago –

Marian Please stop going on about poor old men. There were undoubtedly poor old men among the victims. Go on about them, for a change.

Cressida You do believe he's guilty. (*Silence.*) I think we should forgive and forget, we're Christians, aren't we?

From somewhere, Roman's voice, moaning and crying.

Julian Where the hell is he now? (*Goes to look.*) He's by Rosie's grave – and there's a bloke taking a photograph of him – (*yelling*) You! Get off my land! And Roman! Shut it! (*He returns to the others.*) If they try that again, I'm going to call the police –

Cressida Did anyone hear what I said? Is anyone listening to me? I'm the one that's being punished here, I'm the one. Listen to me. I said, we're Christians. We should forgive and forget.

(handwritten annotation: sound the melodrama.)

Marian I'm going to take you to task again, Mrs Field. Firstly, we are not the ones to forgive. Only the victims can forgive. We can't do that for them. We have a duty to the dead –

Cressida Now she's preaching again – *she is.*

Marian And how dare we forget this most terrible event in human history? We forget it at our peril. Because if we forget it, it'll happen again. And if we forget it we allow those who now deny it to triumph. Those who say the

Holocaust never happened are accessories after the fact.

Cressida You can't go on and on for ever and ever. It's all ancient history –

Julian Yes, but we like to remember our history, don't we, we just don't want other people to remember theirs.

Marian smiles.

Do you know what I read the other day? In the 12th century we set fire to Jews, and the great Christian heroes of the crusades always started off on their journey with a Jew-burning party – (*He laughs.*)

Cressida Shut up, Julian, shut up, shut up! You know nothing about it, 12th century, the Crusades –

Marian rises. Cressida confronts her.

Come on, admit it, this is revenge, revenge, that's all it is, nothing short of revenge. That's what they want. That's what the Jews want, revenge.

Marian (*dangerously calm*) Please be careful what you say now, Mrs Field.

Cressida Why should I be careful? You know it's true. Jesus taught forgiveness, and Jehovah taught vengeance. That's the difference. That's why Romka was in the dock today. They want revenge –

Roman shuffles in. He has been drinking.

Julian Roman, what are you doing here? You promised Cressy you'd rest –

Roman Can't stay alone. I am cold inside. I am frightened man. Morning, noon, night, damned. I stand in sunshine, put my face to sun, feel no heat, but in my heart, winter, ice, deep, deep frost. We are in trap made by devil, so say me Father Alexei –

Julian Oh Christ –

Roman Yes, Christ, Christ, where is my Christ? I cry to
my Maureen, speak to Christ for me. I am old. I have
hard life. I have no one.

Julian Stop feeling sorry for yourself.

Roman cries.

Cressida Look at him. Isn't that enough for them? Look
at him. Isn't that enough revenge?

No response.

I'm waiting for an answer, Mrs Stone. Have you run out
of arguments. Has your First in Philosophy let you down?
Has your well of beautifully structured sentences and
exquisitely enunciated thoughts run dry? Jesus taught forgiveness and Jehovah taught vengeance is what I said.
You people want revenge, that's all you people want –

Marian You people? Who *do* you mean?

Cressida My father gave his life for you people.

Silence.

Marian Mrs Field, I'm going to give it to you hard and
I'm going to give it to you straight. When the Germans
elected Adolf Hitler, a human being by the way, many of
them said that he offered hope for their future. The great
mass flocked to him. Not evil people, but ordinary, good,
Christian folk –

Cressida I was waiting for that, yes, yes, good Christian
folk –

Marian You asked me, I'm going to tell you and you're
going to listen. They all knew that at the heart of what
Adolf Hitler offered was hatred of the Jews. He made no
secret of it. On the contrary, he proclaimed it loudly and

79

[Handwritten annotations in margins:]
sympathy – everyone is both familiar and hateful
sometimes Julian actually makes sense.
That's not what this is about, Cress.
Harwood is great at distributing
↳ Really? From the start? And also, it wasn't just the Jews who the Nazis murdered.

clearly. They knew but chose to ignore it –

Cressida No more, please, no more, this is my house –

Marian Hatred of the Jews was the heart of Nazism. That was the poison. And most of them had already drunk deep. The poison had been fed to them by their parents and their parents' parents, and untold generations, so that they had become immune. The hatred of the Jews is a cultural norm in our civilization, cultivated and allowed to mature for over two thousand years. Don't drink any more of the poison, Mrs Field. I would have thought your father died for his king and country. He died so that I can practise my law, so that you are able to study for your degree and that your husband can make money and go to the opera.

Roman How can she make this mistake?

Julian What are you on about?

Roman Sister Sophia, how can she make such mistake? She say I kill my sister. This is not right. This is not true. I was not there. She remembers wrong. How can she say I kill my sister?

Silence. Marian starts to collect up her things.

Cressida You've only one defence, Romka, darling. There is only one defence. You deny it. Not just these charges against you, but the whole Jewish fantasy –

Julian Cressida –

Cressida How do we know it really happened? Never mind your sister, Romka, how do we know that all these millions were murdered at all?

Stillness.

I want an answer. I'm one of your accessories after the

fact. We deny it. <u>That's our defence</u>, Romka. We deny it. It never happened. None of it. Ever.

> *Marian with great suddenness and severity cracks Cressida across the face with the back of her hand. Cressida is at first stunned. So are the others. Then Cressida sinks slowly to the ground. Julian rushes to her, holds and comforts her. Marian turns to find Roman, standing before her, fists clenched, trembling. Marian bows her head, covers her face. No one moves. Cressida weeps. Roman goes to her, kneels beside her, holds her hand. Just the sound of Cressida's painful sobs.*
>
> *The lights fade to blackout.*

Cressida's character development – from liberal(ish) Gender Studies student to Holocaust denial.

It becomes clear that this play actually has nothing to do with Roman. Romka is just the catalyst that allows us to see the degrees of morality in Cressida, Julian, and Marian.

Made in the USA
San Bernardino, CA
14 July 2013